WHERE ON EARTH IS THE
KINGDOM
OF HEAVEN?
A Contemplation

MARCIA E. HAVARIS

BALBOA.
PRESS

A DIVISION OF HAY HOUSE

Scriptures taken from the Holy Bible, New International Version®, NIV®. Copyright © 1973, 1978, 1984, 2011 by Biblica, Inc.™ Used by permission of Zondervan. All rights reserved worldwide. www.zondervan.com The "NIV" and "New International Version" are trademarks registered in the United States Patent and Trademark Office by Biblica, Inc.™

Balboa Press books may be ordered through booksellers or by contacting:

Balboa Press
A Division of Hay House
1663 Liberty Drive
Bloomington, IN 47403
www.balboapress.com
1 (877) 407-4847

Because of the dynamic nature of the Internet, any web addresses or links contained in this book may have changed since publication and may no longer be valid. The views expressed in this work are solely those of the author and do not necessarily reflect the views of the publisher, and the publisher hereby disclaims any responsibility for them.

The author of this book does not dispense medical advice or prescribe the use of any technique as a form of treatment for physical, emotional, or medical problems without the advice of a physician, either directly or indirectly. The intent of the author is only to offer information of a general nature to help you in your quest for emotional and spiritual well-being. In the event you use any of the information in this book for yourself, which is your constitutional right, the author and the publisher assume no responsibility for your actions.

Any people depicted in stock imagery provided by Getty Images are models, and such images are being used for illustrative purposes only.
Certain stock imagery © Getty Images.

Print information available on the last page.

ISBN: 978-1-5043-9522-9 (sc)
ISBN: 978-1-5043-9524-3 (hc)
ISBN: 978-1-5043-9523-6 (e)

Library of Congress Control Number: 2018900516

Balboa Press rev. date: 03/14/2018

TABLE OF CONTENTS

Also by Marcia Havaris
Volume 1 Poetry - To My Parents
Volume 2 Poetry - Friends
Volume 3 Poetry - Love
Journey to the Center of You
Love Is

Spoken-Word Audio

You Know Me
Forest Meditation
The Voice of Silence
Christmas Meditations
Advent * Christmas * New Year
Meditations for Centering and Healing

Vocal CDs

A Bouquet of Roses
Christmas CD – "What Would I Give Him?"

Visit Marcia at
SoulPoems2go.com
Inspired Poems
Inspirational Writings

DEDICATION

This book is lovingly dedicated to you and all those who
ponder thoughts about the Kingdom of Heaven

EPIGRAPH

"When we find and realize the Kingdom in ourselves,
we experience a growing wholeness,
an increasing sense of the meaning
of our individual personality,
a realization of new and creative energies,
and an expanding consciousness.
This leads us beyond our individual ego-existence
to an experience
with a transcendent source of life
and to a creative life in the social sphere.

The Kingdom
involves the realization of our personalities
according to the inner plan established within us by God;
hence, the unfolding of a Self
that predates and transcends the ego."

John A. Sanford
The Kingdom Within

PREFACE

"Thy Kingdom come,
Thy Will be done
On earth as it is in Heaven"
Matthew 6:9-13

Reading these lines from the Lord's Prayer
created a deep desire within me
to explore Kingdom thoughts.
So, a few years ago,
I began to write down these inspirations
as I received them.

These are thoughts upon which to muse and ponder.
My desire is to open a door to Mystery
and allow a pathway of exploration
to unfold.

I invite you to walk this path with me
and to explore your own thoughts
regarding the Kingdom of Heaven.

INTRODUCTION

We do not have to wait until we experience physical death
to enter the Kingdom of Heaven.

God's Kingdom is both a destination and a state of being.

Kingdom Living is a not a reward we earn,
rather it is a choice we make

****

"Heaven is in the heart.
They will look for it in vain who look elsewhere.
In no outward place will the soul find Heaven
until it finds it within itself".

James Allen
All These Things Added

"God's Kingdom isn't something you can see.
There is no use saying 'Look! Here it is' or 'Look! There it is.'
God's Kingdom is here with[in] you."

Luke 17: 20, 21

Perhaps the Kingdom of Heaven
is not just a place where we go upon our physical death.
Rather it is how we live in the present world
once we realize we are Spirit
in the here and now.

We do not have to wait until we "die" to be (re)united with God.

We can choose right now
to die to the illusion of being separate from God
and find ourselves
instantly connected once again to His Spirit.

By simply choosing
to believe that we are connected,
the Holy Spirit will flow through our lives freely.
The Spirit is always ready and waiting.
It is we who are blinded
by our own sight,
lacking true Vision.

When we invite the Holy Spirit of God
to illuminate us within
we can begin to see the Kingdom

When we allow our mind
to connect with God's mind
we begin to share in Kingdom thoughts.

When we open our Heart
to the unconditional love of God,
we find ourselves born into the Kingdom,
where we can become Pure Love-
one with God.

The Kingdom of Heaven
is like a tiny seed which,
when planted, grows into a beautiful flower.

As we empty ourselves of the things of this world
the Kingdom of Heaven grows
and expands within us
until it finally becomes our full reality.

It blooms
and gently breaks forth into our life
as the Truth of Love
which sets us free.

As we rid ourselves of all we think to be real
we discover unspeakable love
blossoming in the soil of our soul.

"Then Jesus asked,
'What is the kingdom of God like?
What shall I compare it to?
It is like a mustard seed,
which a man took and planted in his garden.
It grew and became a tree,
and the birds perched in its branches.'"

Luke 13:18-19

Living in the Kingdom brings enriched experience
It transforms our lives from dull to meaningful,
from tepid to intense, from fearful to loving
…now freely welcoming mystery.

Kingdom living
moves us from a place of living by rules
into a place of experiencing the miraculous.

All things ordinary
are enhanced by extraordinary beauty and vitality
in the Kingdom.

Even the tiniest mustard seeds in our lives
expand and develop into magnificent trees
the branches of which become home for the birds
of life's great experiences.

The Kingdom of Heaven waits quietly for us to seek it.
It does not attempt to draw us in with noise and glitter.
It makes no appeal to our physical senses.

It merely *IS*...
open,
serene,
waiting,
ready to embrace all who are seeking.

The Kingdom of Heaven
bursts forth with the infinite power and grace
of unconditional Love.

Love
which suspends judgment in every moment –

Love
which perceives purity and perfection in all things –

Love
which shines light into a dark world.

This unconditional Love
holds the key that unlocks the Kingdom
for all humanity

Where there is Love
There is God

Where there is God
there is the Kingdom

"And the peace of God, which transcends all understanding, will guard your hearts and your minds in Christ Jesus."

Philippians 4:7

The Kingdom of God is Peace within

– a Peace that passes all understanding –

a Peace that needs not defend itself.

For the Truth needs no defense,
and it is the Truth
which provides this Peace.

The Kingdom of Heaven is Spirit.

Nothing can prevail against it.
It is unshakable.
It is Truth.
It can never be lost
but it may be hidden from our sight
by what we choose to observe.

We experience the physical world around us
through our five senses.
Yet these senses are connected to our body, not our spirit,
so the world we perceive through them is not real.
The body can only perceive another form
that vibrates slowly enough to appear solid.

But our spirit, our inner consciousness,
our sixth sense, our "third eye",
experiences on the level of the Spirit.
It is this which is real and eternal.

As we open our inner vision
we then connect to the great River of Spirit,
flowing through our center…

...When we choose to step into this River
we then have a Life which flows freely...
carried by the energy of Spirit
and not bound by the physical,
or inhibited by the material world.

As we move into the River
we become one with the momentum of creative essence.
We connect to the Universal Spirit and Energy –
we experience God.
This is why Christ taught us to let go of
attachment to material things.
Do not attach value to something that has no real (eternal) worth
for these things are simply of the material world.
Therefore they are not real and merely serve a finite purpose.

We can only enter the Kingdom of God
when we release our attachment to the finite
and hold on to that which serves a higher purpose,
thus allowing our energy to connect to the flowing energy of life.

The Kingdom is not a thing to be sought after.

Moreover we can but allow a place within ourselves
to invite the Kingdom to grow and expand.

We choose whether or not to enter the Kingdom
and all our choices will either create the Kingdom within
or leave us wandering aimlessly as we seek outside of our self
for a kingdom that is not real.

Any external kingdom that the ego attempts to create
is mere illusion and distraction.
It is ego's nature to turn our vision away from seeing God.

When we let go of the illusion that we can
find the Kingdom outside of our self
it is then possible to discover
that the keys were in our hands all along
and we are free to open the door
and permit ourselves to enter the Kingdom.

The Kingdom of Heaven
is at the deepest part of the River of Life.

We cannot enter the Kingdom
by standing on the shore.

We must be willing to jump into the River
and to plunge into its depths.

We must open ourselves
to allow the River to flow into us
so that we experience life fully.

Then with faith we let go and trust the River
as it carries us to the Kingdom.

This great River of Life
flows through the centre of our being.

It is not enough for us to stand on the banks
and watch the river flow by.

We must enter the water
to experience the River,
and know what it is to be part of the River.

In this way our longing for the Kingdom
becomes active seeking,
which in turn propels us through the River
becoming one with the current of God
drawing us into the Kingdom.

Stepping off the material bank
into the Spiritual River of Life
and merging with the stream,
we find our life becomes more effortless
and we no longer have physical blocks
impeding our flow.

As we come upon a rock
which appears in the river,
we are free to move around it
or we may choose to stand upon it
and take time to reflect upon our life.

When we are ready,
we may let go of the rock
and slip back into the flow of life in the spirit.

When we try to collect the rocks
and dwell in the memory of what they represent,
our life-flow can become slow and stagnant.

All the rocks we have collected bog us down
and we feel pulled into the dense material world…

...Only when we choose to release the rocks
do we find ourselves flowing easily, once more,
upon the energy of Spirit.

The rocks can serve as stepping-stones
to help us move along the River of Life.
Used in this way we can learn from them.
We can gain a new perspective
and grow and expand our inner awareness.
But if we see the rocks as obstacles to our path
we will remain blocked and stuck.

The only way around them is to step back into the flow
and leave the rocks behind us.
We need not push against them
nor should we carry them with us.
They are lessons but not limits.
So we can observe, learn and move on.

"If we think we have any kingdom other than that of God's, we're standing outside the kingdom."

Living The Course Pg. 119

When we surrender to God we are surrendering to Spirit
and letting go of anything which appears to bind us
or block us from our experience of Spirit.
Whatever we hold onto is what we value
and what we value is that in which we have placed our hope.

We will find ourselves stuck in the experience of the unreal
if we are depending on the material world
to provide our strength, support, pleasure, hope and life.

We lose the frequency of our connection to Spirit
and at that point we experience the illusion
of being separate from God.

As we detach from things of the material world
we find our frequency once again vibrating at a higher level
and we have an experience of Spiritual Energy
flowing through us.
Our frequency is restored
and we rediscover our open connection to God.

"The Kingdom of God is within you."
Luke 17:21

At the entrance to the Kingdom
we must put behind ego and all its limitations.
We must leave our old life - our old self.

As we enter the Kingdom
we take up the Spirit and its fullness of creativity.
We don our new self and step into a new life.

We leave all limiting ideas and beliefs behind
and take on the unlimited thoughts of Faith and Love.

As we turn our focus and attention to God
we experience our spirit rising free of the self which would bind it.
And we enter a new and glorious Self
which shares with Christ the garment of righteousness.

What was not eternal has died
and what is eternal has been raised to life.

"You are the light of the world.
A town built on a hill cannot be hidden.
Neither do people light a lamp and put it under a bowl.
Instead they put it on its stand,
and it gives light to everyone in the house.
In the same way, let your light shine before others,
that they may see your good deeds and glorify your Father in heaven."

Matthew 5:14-16

The Kingdom of Heaven is like a generator – a source of energy.
It is the origin of ALL loving energy.
If we stay connected to this source of loving energy
we will find the light of the Kingdom shining through us.
The Light will shine through every aspect of our life
just as the bright beams shine through
the windows of a lighthouse.

Our thoughts, speech, actions, the look in our eyes,
our every movement reflect the light within.
Our mind, joined with the mind of God,
becomes the beacon atop the lighthouse.
We will want our light to shine so the world may see it
and be drawn to God.

If we are the light of the world
then the Kingdom of Heaven is within us.
As each one of us allows the light of God to shine through us
the light dispels fear and darkness
and the Kingdom of Heaven expands.

One day all darkness will be gone
as the light fills the Universe
and we will dwell
in the Kingdom of God
forever.

"Ask and it will be given to you.
Seek and ye shall find.
Knock and it shall be opened unto you."

Matthew 7:7

Kingdom Living
is not about living apart from others.

The longer you dwell in the Kingdom
the more you yearn for others
to join in and share the experience.

As the Kingdom fills us,
it expands
and gradually makes all our walls transparent.

Where once we remained closed and distant from others,
the Kingdom now radiates through the transparent walls
and shines its light into the world around us.

So we seek the Kingdom within
and upon discovering and dwelling in the Kingdom,
it then becomes our reality
and we do not remain within
but rather turn ourselves inside out
and once again enter the world -
now reunited with the Kingdom.

"But seek first his kingdom and his righteousness,
and all these things will be given to you as well.
Therefore do not worry about tomorrow,
for tomorrow will worry about itself.
Each day has enough trouble of its own."

Matthew 6:33-34

When we seek the Kingdom of God
our desires begin to change and evolve
as we find ourselves more in a place of love.

We discover we have full access to an abundant life.

Flowing abundance which increasingly serves all humanity
becomes our heart's desire as we seek the Kingdom.

We have less of a desire to *have the* abundance
and more desire to *be* the abundance for others.

Releasing our fearful illusion of need,
we become more aware of the loving truth of abundance.

Only His Kingdom is eternal.
Only His Kingdom is pure Love.
Nothing else is real.

Any who builds apart from the Kingdom of God builds in vain.

We put a lot of time and effort
into living in such a way that we believe
will result in us going to heaven when we die.

But what if we could live in such a way
as to experience Heaven on earth right here and now?

There is nothing that we *need!*

The Kingdom has all riches
of the Universe within it.

All the Eternal treasures,
which are ours in the Kingdom,
satisfy so completely as to eliminate
the sense of void or need.

As we are increasingly filled with the Kingdom
the Universe responds to the abundance in our souls
and we begin to experience fullness
more and more

When we are outside of the Kingdom of God,
striving to create kingdoms of our own making,
the Universe recognizes lack
and reflects emptiness
which leaves us with unfulfilled feelings
and continuously striving for something more…

When we create the illusion of kingdoms
apart from the Kingdom of God
we will never be satisfied,
for nothing is real except the Kingdom of God.

*"Except ye be converted; and become as little children,
ye shall not enter into the Kingdom of heaven.
Whosoever therefore shall humble himself as this little child,
the same is greatest in the Kingdom of Heaven.
And whoso shall receive one such little child in my name receiveth me."*

Matthew 18: 3-5

The Kingdom calls us to be true to ourselves
and to develop pure relationships
with others and with God.

We need not look to any other
for our fulfillment or validation
as individuals.

As we seek to understand ourselves
both consciously and unconsciously
we are able to build stronger relationships.

As we become whole, integrated persons,
healthy relationships become our reality.

Only as our inner person is strong
and we know ourselves well
are we then able
to have meaningful relationships
with others.

Life is full of choices.

Every decision we make
moves us closer to the Kingdom
or draws us away from the Kingdom.

We may always choose Love or a loving response.

Making Kingdom Choices

In Heaven there is no pain -
so bring healing to every situation
Now

In Heaven Peace reigns -
so choose peace in every moment
Now

In Heaven there is no illness -
so make healthy choices in every way
Now

In Heaven there is no darkness -
so allow your Light to shine everywhere
Now

In Heaven there is only kindness,
consideration and compassion -
so be kind, considerate and compassionate
Now

In Heaven there is unconditional and non-judgmental acceptance
of all people and creatures -
so suspend all judgment and extend acceptance
Now

In Heaven Love prevails -
So be loving in every way
Now

Embracing the Kingdom
heals our perception,
transporting us to a new reality.

Everything looks new
yet nothing has physically changed…

Everywhere we look
we see a world
transformed by our Kingdom view.

Kingdom vitality permeates our daily living.
Kingdom wisdom infuses our thoughts.
Clear Kingdom direction guides our actions.
Our words breathe Kingdom joy into our relationships
Our whole life radiates Kingdom Love.

You are invited to step into the Kingdom
Now.

The Kingdom of God is an interior expanse
where all humanity meets at its center.

The Kingdom of Heaven
is vaster than all the universes
in the physical realm.
For it is without measure -
it is spaceless and timeless.
It is indescribable for it is LOVE.
And the finite mind
knows not how to describe the infinite.

The Kingdom of Love was created by God
and is therefore more real
than any temporal kingdom we may construct.

God's creations are perfect and remain in Him.

The creative energy of His Love sustains all that is.

There is nothing created
that did not come from God
and anything that is not from God
is not real (has no eternal value).

Everything you need is present within you.

However you have created a superficial illusion around you -
a temporary manifestation
which distracts you from your true essence.
Looking around,
your vision is drawn outward,
and you forget to look within.

Release the outward manifestations!

Close your eyes
that you might see truth within.
Close your ears
that you might hear truth within.
Close your heart to temporal desires
that you might find true love within.

Then you can realize that all is within you
and now you lack nothing....

…we can have everything we desire
and yet what we most want and need is to desire nothing.

In the moment we no longer yearn for inconsequential things
we discover that those things never really existed.

Instead of reaching out for illusive cobwebs
we can sit at peace within our self;
our hands resting
contentedly upon our lap
palms opened and facing upward,
ready to receive the total nothingness
which is our true deepest longing.

We need no longer be part of the race or the chase.
for we finally realize there was no race or chase
and that all that was required of us
was to wait,
silently,
in love,
and to know our self.

We can experience the Kingdom of God
when we infuse loving attention
into mundane, ordinary tasks.

We can begin to find a sacred quality
hidden
within a daily duty or a simple act of kindness.

Directing loving attention into our daily activities
produces riches in the Kingdom within our soul.

If our spirit is not tangible
why would we search for a tangible kingdom?

As our spirit is an extension of God's Spirit,
so our true dwelling place is in God.

As we come to recognize who we truly are
we will realize that we have never left the Kingdom.

We must first gain clear vision
and open our inner sight -
not look for the Kingdom
with clouded perception.

There is nowhere we need to "*go*"
to arrive at the Kingdom.
But simply to "*let go*"
of all that which we have been trying to hold onto,
allowing it all to be released
so we are free to" be" in the Kingdom.

We bring nothing but our essence through the Kingdom door -
for in the Kingdom our only need
is to experience union with our Creator
and in reconnecting with the Divine
we discover that we are everything,
have everything,
yet need nothing.

It is up to us to bring Heaven to Earth.
We cannot expect God
to fix our problems in this universe
if we continue doing the things
that created undesirable circumstances in the first place.

If we want to experience God
in the "here and now"
then we must make space
in our experiences of me and thou.

We cannot continue to block Love
and expect to experience healing, peace and joy in our lives.

Recognize that Love is what we seek
in every moment
and choose to let go of everything
that would stand in the way of Love

To experience the Kingdom in our heart
we are invited to look at things differently,
adopt a new perspective,
change direction,
shift our view.
and see things in a new way.

We do not have to wait for the Kingdom to appear.

The Kingdom of God is here now
and waits for us to enter its gates.

The gates to the Kingdom
are adorned with
Love,
Joy,
Peace,
Forgiveness
and
Grace.

When we allow these attributes of the Spirit
to permeate our lives,
then the gates to the Kingdom
swing wide open.

When we judge or criticize another
for what we perceive to be negative characteristics,
we buy into an illusion,
thereby reinforcing a seemingly apparent reality
which is exactly that which we so desire to change.

In attempting to change another person first,
we extend our focus into the illusion of separateness
thereby delaying the miracle of transformation.

In so doing
we step outside of the Kingdom ways.

To dispel the illusion
we must see others as they really are:
pure, holy, loving children of God,
powerful, energetic, spiritual beings
also striving to remember their true essence.

We are not separate from anyone or anything.

As we allow the transformative miracle
of love and total forgiveness
to work in us,
it then manifests in the world around us.

At a Kingdom level
if something is true about one,
it is true about all.
At deepest level of the Spirit we are One –
pure love, perfect beings.
We choose to experience in our human form,
and between the level of the Spirit
and the surface of humanity,
dwells all possibility.

Each of us has the potential to be or experience anything.

We must be careful, therefore, not to judge others,
for it is only in an area with which we do not wrestle
that we feel ourselves to be greater or stronger.
But if we look honestly within ourselves
we will quickly see
that which others find easy to judge within us.

So we must look at each other
with loving forgiveness
and thereby find ourselves gently forgiven
and once again experience the Kingdom.

For where your treasure is, there your heart will be also."

Matthew 6:19-21

There is no room for hatred or opposition
in the Kingdom of God.
What we hate we oppose
and being in opposition
is a form of bondage.

We are only free to enter the Kingdom
when we relinquish judgment, rejection, hatred and opposition
and don the garments of love and peace.

We must also love ourselves,
for this is the manner in which
we allow the creative Spirit of God
to freely express Itself through us.
Denying the Spirit of God within ourselves
we deny the very creative energy of God
which brings us to life and teaches us how to love.

This is the lesson of love
which prepares us for the Kingdom.

Perfection is not a prerequisite to finding the Kingdom.
What is required is a heart open to love -
open to receive God's Love -
open to give love to itself and others.

Love does not label or judge,
it receives and accepts.
Love comes with childlike faith and trust
As we are able, once again, to become like children
we find entrance into the Kingdom.

A child believes with his heart
and does not rationalize or analyze with his head.
He is open to receive with a faith that is pure.

The Kingdom is like a Heavenly Feast
to which everyone who is hungry is invited.

No one is turned away.

The table is spread with the Food of Life
and the water is drawn from the River of Life.

All who share in the Feast
enter into a soul community
where love is freely expressed
and the heart of the experience is joy.

At the head of the table is God,
the Source and Provider of the Feast.

As God serves the spiritual Food and Drink
it is passed on and shared by all.

The more it is shared the more He gives.

No one tries to stop the abundant flow of nourishment
for everyone knows that there is no end to the Source...

...The invitation to the Feast goes out to everyone.
It is up to each of us to choose how we respond.

The Feast is ready and waiting
for all who will enter through the door of Love.

As we share in the Kingdom Feast
we realize that
although the thoughts and beliefs we bring
to the Feast are different for each one of us
the experience of the Kingdom Elements
is the same.

It is not by serving ourselves
that we will find satisfaction-
for that approach keeps us
in "starvation mode"
-always wanting more
and never feeling fulfilled...

…When with love and compassion we reach out
to meet the needs of others and to serve community,
then all manner of abundance
flows through us and we are nourished.

As we feed others we are fed.
As we love others we are loved.
As we forgive others we are forgiven.

As long as we remain in the presence of God,
the Feast continues.
But the Feast is intended to be shared
and it is in sharing
that the abundance increases.

Community brings the awareness
that we were not created to be separate.
In sharing the elements of the Feast
we are drawn into communion with God
and with one another…

…Nothing we hold onto and try to keep for ourselves is truly ours.

Nothing we give to others in the spirit of pure Love
ever really leaves us.

Upon entering through the Kingdom door
we find ourselves in the innermost chamber of our heart
and on the throne sits the King of Love.

The Food of the Feast
is the Bread of Life
served
on a platter of Love.

The Drink of the Feast
is the Water of Life
poured out lavishly
from the vial of Truth.

It is our experience of the Kingdom,
which is universal and can be shared by all.

Only Love surrounds us now.
We are filled and the Feast flows through us.

"Blessed is the one who will eat at the feast in the kingdom of God."

Luke 14:15

Come to the Kingdom
with an open heart,
an open mind,
open arms.

Come to the Kingdom
ready to receive from the King.

Come to the Kingdom
prepared to embrace Kingdom Living
and come knowing that as you do
you will embrace all humanity
and will share the invitation to the Feast.

If we desire to experience the Kingdom now
we must make Kingdom choices consciously.
including
What we eat
What we drink
Where we go
What we listen to
What we look at
With whom we spend time
What we do

We will experience the Kingdom
if what we choose is the Kingdom.

One manner of determining
which experiences will draw us into the Kingdom,
or draw the Kingdom into us, is to ask ourselves:

Does this come from a place of love?
Does this encourage?
Does this bring peace?
Does this allow for creativity?
Does this foster community and sharing?
Does this bring unconditional love to me and to all around me?

Living without God is like dwelling in death.

But dying to the ego-promoting self brings new life
through regeneration of the soul.

It is in dying that we find life
and in living that we find there is no more death.

Kingdom music
is songs of love and forgiveness -
but not as we know or sing it.
God's love is unconditional and His forgiveness perfect.

God does not recognize our errors or sins.

He sees only the perfection of His creation.
In His perfect Love for us
is also total forgiveness.

He does not wait for us to come and ask forgiveness -
His Love is perfect
and therein lies our true forgiveness.

We need only access God's Love to be forgiven -
restored to the perfection He created.

Stream of Life

The gentle, flowing stream of life
would wash away all pain and strife,
would bathe us in its cool delight,
would soothe us with its warming light,
would mingle with our tears of pain,
refreshing us with love again,
would fill our hearts with joy's desire
and cleanse us with its purest fire.

Deep within, this river flows.
The silent witness in us knows
its grace-filled Source is God alone,
Who dwells within each sacred tone.
So sing, and see your prayers ascend
to the Kingdom without end
and find, within this river sweet,
your joy,
your love,
your life,
complete.

The Kingdom of God is not someplace we go.

It is within us
waiting for us to let go
of all that is not of God,
all illusion and error,
all unbelief and doubt.

For these things have no substance,
no eternal value,
and are therefore not real.

Once we are able to release these
we discover within us a heavenly state,
a temple, wherein dwells the God of Love and all that is.

We find the kingdom of God overflowing into our life.
We find the love of God becoming our life.

"Be still and know that I am God."
Psalm 46:10

The Kingdom of God is "in you"
for you are God's creation
and where you are God is present
and where God is His kingdom is also.

We seek to rid ourselves
of anything that blocks our vision of the Kingdom,
anything that attempts to block the Truth
and stands in the way of Love.

When we choose to "be still"
we can once again know that God is.
And the great "I Am" presence
reveals Itself to our inner sight.

In that stillness
we can know that God is
and we can receive the knowing.

And as we give greater expression
to the Kingdom of heaven within,
we also begin to experience an outer reality
which manifests love, peace and truth.

You are the temple of God.
At your center is God's altar.
Allow the Shekinah Glory to
radiate out from your center
filling every aspect of your life with brilliance.

Shine on and be the best you can be.

The Temple of Wisdom

We enter the temple of Wisdom
and far across the other side we see GOD,
a beautiful, glorious, all-radiant light,
drawing us lovingly towards Itself.

The light is like a long, open hallway
~ all light & love ~
and as we enter the light we find our space,
the space that fits us perfectly,
the hollow that was there from when we first went out

And now we return to fill that hollow,
~ one by one ~
each person, each living creature finds its place in GOD,
feeling an unsurpassable joy and deepest peace.

All longing ceases and contentment fills each being.

Finally, as the last hollow is filled,
GOD lovingly embraces Himself,
embracing within Himself all the galaxies and universes
and every living being, created and uncreated,
all returned to the SOURCE,
the Beginning & the End,
and He laughs.
His joy overflows.

LIGHT fills Itself
and flows out into Itself again.

"When you finally discover the Kingdom
you live with a transcendent vision.
You are in a heavenly kingdom,
that is, a realm of meaning
not limited to the unconscious assumptions
of the average, modern person,
such as success, money, sexual dominance and self-interest.
You are in the world
but not dominated by its unconscious values.

Heaven is a spiritual dimension,
the sphere of the Father,
a realm connected to daily life and yet beyond it.

When you find yourself in the Kingdom,
you will be in a different world,
though at the factual level everything will be the same.

The Kingdom is translucent and empty.
You don't see it in itself,
but you see the world altered by it."

from <u>Writing In The Sand.</u> Thomas Moore

To enter into the Kingdom of God
we must shed our external façade
and cultivate the inner person.

Outward pretence must be shed.

It is necessary to go deep within
and recognize all that we find there,
then bring it to the light.

As we do this
we can make meaningful decisions
about what to keep and what to discard.

Once we cleanse and purify our heart
and the inner person has been made whole
our outer masks are no longer necessary
that we once wore in an attempt
to present ourselves
as something we were not.

For then, the inner person will shine forth:
the outer now being a true reflection of the inner.

Only then are we free to enter the Kingdom
for we have left behind our unnecessary pretences
and we are no longer divided within ourselves.

The Light now dispels the darkness
as the Kingdom door opens wide.

"But the fruit of the Spirit
is love,
joy,
peace,
forbearance,
kindness,
goodness,
faithfulness,
gentleness
and self-control.

Against such things there is no law."

Galatians 5:22-23

The Kingdom of Heaven is within.

Our souls dwell in the Kingdom.

So it is that we must go within
to know and experience
the dwelling place of our soul.

Our spirit is connected to the Spirit of God
and through that connection
runs the current of God's Love and creative power.

It is necessary to choose
to keep the connection strong and clear of corruption
if we desire to experience oneness with God.

As we turn our sight inward we gain stronger "insight"
which leads to the dwelling place of our soul.

As we dwell in the Kingdom
our life becomes free
from anger, fear, suspicion, jealousy,
caprice, anxiety and grief.

Our lives then manifest
the fruit of the Spirit-
'love, joy, peace, long-suffering, kindness, goodness,
faithfulness, meekness, temperance, self-control'.
[Galatians 5:22-23]

The Sacred Self

The Sacred Self
its soul does know

By breath itself
Its life does flow.

There is no start
Nor place to end.

The Breath, into a circle
bends.

So come into this circle now
And in your centre kneel and bow
To God who gives life and sustains
All those who, in Him, do remain.

Dwelling *in* self does not mean dwelling *by* self.

It is *within*
that we make contact with the Source of our being.

Connecting to God within
enables us to bring His Kingdom
into our outer reality.

The Kingdom of God is not a place we go
in an attempt to alienate ourselves from the world.

Rather it is a place to which we go
in order to discover great treasure
that we may share with the world.

We seek the Kingdom not for ourselves alone
But with the hope that in seeking
we will find that which connects all hearts
as one.

"Blessed are the poor in spirit:
for theirs is the Kingdom of Heaven"

Matthew 5:3

In the illusion of humanity
"we" claim to be something "they" are not,
or that "they" are something "we" are not.

And yet, in truth,
whatever we observe in another exists within ourselves
or we would not be able to see it in another.

So we are wise to look within, in all humility,
choosing to keep only love and release all else.

In so doing,
we may then see pure love in everyone we meet.

So do not judge; only observe and love.

Forgiveness is the path to pure love.
One cannot love whom one has not forgiven.

When we feel blocked from love,
we can be sure we are holding un-forgiveness
in some corner of our heart.

Open the windows and release all darkness,
so the divine light may enter
and fill your being
with the energetic, healing power
of pure, holy love.

The Kingdom of Heaven begins to appear
as we recognize that we have been trying to live inside out.

When we turn our thinking right side out
and allow our inner vision to be ignited
we start to experience clarity of vision.

This is not the vision of the world as we "know" it,
rather, it is the insight into the realm of the Eternal
where only those thoughts of right-mindedness dwell.

The key to the Kingdom is Love.

The Kingdom is Love.

Only as we find and acknowledge all parts of ourselves
can healing transformation take place.

As all things are brought to Divine Light
we can become whole once again.

Christ's love within
heals all division
and the flower of unity springs up into new life.

The separated self is an illusion
and must find its wholeness once again.

Shining a light into the darkness
allows us to find that which was lost.

The light of Christ would reveal to us
everything we are
and the life of Christ within
enables us to experience our oneness.

Being one with Christ we are one with ourselves
and then become part of the one Kingdom of God
which embraces all as one.

Humanity is like a sea of flameless candles.

As each one of us allows the holy fire of God
to light our candle
the flame of God's love will catch and spread
until all the candles are lit
and every flame burns brightly for God.

The candles may appear
to be separate and individual
but once the flames are lit
the fire becomes one.

There are no defining edges
to the flames.

Fire joins fire
and becomes one eternal Flame
burning as an extension
of the God-flame.

When we choose peace
it becomes possible for those around us to choose peace.

When we hold love within our heart
we open a pathway to allow love to flow from us and to us.
We also create energy in our lives
that encourages others to be more loving.

Anything upon which we focus our attention expands
and love has the potential
to multiply and magnify beyond measure.

A loving word can cut through years of icy bitterness.
One small act of kindness can dissolve a lifetime of dissent.

Love is so powerful so as to overcome any obstacle.

In essence, Love is all there is,
so as we become Love,
we come to understand
that anything which does not appear as Love,
is an appeal for Love.

The Cathedral is filled with a million hues
and the collective breath merges into one magnificent breath.

The heart of all humanity beats in unison
as it recognizes the rhythm of Creation.

We then become the one Breath and one Heart of the Creator
and are complete in our reunion with Him.

The Cathedral expands
and embraces all that was
and all that is
and all that will be;
embraces all
in the Eternal Now.

Imagine sitting in the center of a darkened Cathedral.

Every time we make a choice to connect with Spirit,
a new ray of light
shines through one of the stained glass windows
and casts its hue upon our soul.

The longer we dwell in a state of desire-less receptivity
the more light filters in through the windows
until eventually
the entire cathedral is flooded
with a glorious, radiant multi-coloured light.

As we continue in the center of the Cathedral,
the light spills effortlessly into our soul
and we become a ray of the Light.

As we become the Light,
the windows open slowly, one by one,
and the Light we have become
shines out into the exterior world around us.

We will desire to maintain our connection
to the Source of this glorious Light
if we are to continue to bring Light to the world around us.

"Love the Lord your God with all your heart
and with all your soul and with all your strength
and with all your mind';
and,
'Love your neighbour as yourself."

Luke 10:27

The Kingdom of Heaven is a collective experience
and cannot be entered into alone.

For when we approach its entrance
we discover that we have brought all humanity with us.

We enter the Kingdom
only as our love expands and embraces all of creation.

If we believe we are separate and stand alone
we will not see the Kingdom
for only as the Love of God pours through us
do we gain true in-sight.

Love does not dwell alone.
Love embraces all and recognizes all within Itself.

We will experience God as we share God with others.

Love is ours as we choose to give Love.

"In your relationships with one another,
have the same mindset as Christ Jesus:"

Philippians 2:5

Let us be transformed into the likeness of Christ
and take on the mind of Christ.
At the moment we choose to do this
we then have "eyes to see" and "ears to hear"

When we look out around us
with our present limited vision
all we see is that
which lies within the path of our physical eye.
We then interpret what we "see"
through a lens of perception,
which is tinted
by experience, memory, thoughts and emotions.

As we turn our glance inward
and are patiently silent
our inner eyes will gradually become accustomed
to a new way of seeing
and we will begin to see that which is real
and holds true meaning.

The expanse of truth,
which lies at the center of our inner being,
is only visible to our inner eye,
the soul,
and can only be seen clearly
through the lens of faith and love....

...Only when we become quiet and still
is it then possible for us
to observe with expanded vision
and without distorted perception.

The Truth begins to dawn upon us
like the soft, first light of day.

And the longer we remain within the silence
the greater grows the light within
until finally we find ourselves basking
in the glorious light of Truth in its fullness.

We become aware
of the expansion within us
and realize, at once,
that the Truth embraces all of humanity
and all of creation
in one beautiful, light-filled circle of Love...

...At that moment
our perception shifts
and we "see" what is true and real
and we become one
with the Eternal embrace of Love.

Everywhere we look we see Beauty
through the eyes of Love -
and all of creation is healed, forgiven,
and brought to salvation
in one glorious moment born of this Eternal Love.

Clouded, partial vision clears.
Our layers of tainted perception lay scattered at our feet,
no longer needed nor desired.

Our emotions have dissolved in love's consuming fire
and no longer hold our heart captive as in a tangled web.

We are free to be
and to see
through the eyes
of Eternity, Truth and Love.

"Jesus said,
'My kingdom is not of this world.
….
But now my kingdom is from another place.'"

John 18:36

The external reflects the internal.

Our inner thoughts and feelings
become evidenced as our outer reality.

Only the inner life is real.

The outward expression is merely that—
a manifestation
whose purpose is to reveal, more clearly,
our inner reality.

Once we recognize our outer expression for what it is, we are then able
to choose a response or to take responsibility for what we are creating.

We can then decide
if we would like to change our thoughts or feelings
and allow our inner reality
to better portray our true spirit.

As we give greater expression to the Kingdom of heaven within,
we begin to experience an outer reality,
which manifests love, peace, and truth.

How we choose to respond to any given situation
is a result of our perception and interpretation
of that circumstance.

When we are conscious
and remember not to judge anyone or anything,
we are no longer bound by our perceptions,
which are not based in reality but rather are merely a sign
of our inner growth and enlightenment.

Then when we become fully enlightened,
we will no longer experience these "perceptions."
We will "know" the Truth and the Truth will set us free.

There is but one Kingdom of Heaven,
divinely expressed through each of us.

There are not many heavenly kingdoms
but there are many rooms within the Kingdom.

Truly as we come to our center
- our soul, our heart -
we find all of humanity there,
awaiting the embrace of Eternal Love.

We cannot truly embrace ourselves
without embracing everything.

Eternal Love is not directed
at a physical, separate manifestation,
rather, Eternal Love
encompasses the magnitude of all creation.

Every illusion of separate entities dissolves
and leaves only the lingering essence
of that which is real within.

A moment of discord
is transformed into an experience of peace
when Love enters
and therein lies the Kingdom.

True love can quiet a raging heart
just as Christ calmed the raging sea.

The authority that comes from knowing oneness with God
Creates faith that can move the mountain.

"Blessed are the pure in heart, for they shall see God"
(in every situation. They shall experience God in every moment.)

Matthew 5:8

We can choose love instead of fear.

Our circumstances may not immediately change
but how we experience them will begin to shift.

With modified perception and increased love in each moment
we experience a heightened level of spiritual vibration.

As our energy begins to vibrate more quickly,
being generated by pure love,
it dispels the apparent darkness
and brings the light of God to our awareness.

We discover that God's Light and Love were always present
for nothing can separate us from the love of God
except our own misaligned thoughts and errors of ego thinking.

Evil that we perceive in the world around us
did not come from God.
God did not create evil or sickness or suffering.

What we perceive as evil
will cease to exist
when we cease to think it
and to project it into our experience.

God is Love and everything He created is Good.

If all thoughts of all people turned to thoughts of God
we would know Heaven on earth.
If all hearts of all people turned to God's heart
we would know the Love of God in every moment.

It is not God who has turned His back on us.
It is we who have walked away from God.

Yet as nothing can separate us from the Love of God
we need only change our mind,
turn around and experience a change of heart.
When we recognize that we cannot find love
by attempting to stand on our own
we find God waiting patiently for us to come home.

God waits with open arms
to welcome us back into the Kingdom experience,
to shower us
with the abundance of His riches in Heaven
and to clothe us with the robe of His Glory.

This reunion is all the richer
after the painful experience of our self-created lack...

...God gifts us with all the treasures of the Kingdom,
not so we should squander them
but that we may share them and bless others.
In so doing we in fact find ourselves
in a place of continual abundance.
Whereas if we hold onto what God gives us, from fear,
we risk losing even that which He has given us.

When we dwell with God
we have no need of anything
as, at all times, we have access to His riches.

In leaving His presence
and loosing our connection to the Source
the abundance becomes seemingly inaccessible.

At that moment
we begin to perceive ourselves
as lacking or suffering
when in fact all we lack
is our connection to that source
which comes from dwelling with God.

We do not need to build a temple- we ARE the Temple.

"Don't you know that you yourselves are God's temple and that God's Spirit dwells in your midst?"

1 Corinthians 3:16

As we draw closer to God,
we become one in the intimacy of
His relationship with all of creation.

We start to feel His heart beating within us.

We are able to hear the whisper of His breath
calling out gently to the beloved.

We feel the passion of His desire
to be united with the beloved.

We see only the beauty in the beloved
as we become one with His vision....

We see as He sees;
hear as He hears;
feel as He feels;
love as He loves.

We lose ourselves in Him
only to find ourselves,
once again,
in all of creation.

As we release our former definition of whom we are,
we find that we are essence,
no longer needing to be defined.

And the Kingdom opens before us.

God,
You are that eternal flame
which burns passionately
at the center of our being.

Your Holy Spirit
is like the golden lava
of a Sacred Volcano
which erupts with joy
and fills our being with the fire of divinity.

I open every crevice of who I am
and ask You to so expand within me
that all that is not You
would be washed away
in the flood of Your holy love.

May there be nothing but You within me.

I yearn for complete oneness with You, oh God,
and know that in that moment,
I will also be one with all humanity,
indeed with all creation.

Are you ready
to enter the Kingdom of God:
to receive the abundant riches of His glory?

What blocks your way?

What mask do you wear?

Why do you delay?

Do you feel unworthy?

Are you afraid?

Do you feel you will have to give up the life you have right now?

Do not be afraid.

The Kingdom brings Peace
and all your fears can melt
in the loving warmth of the Kingdom's fire.

As we toss into the fire all we do not need,
and anything
that would stand in our way of receiving Love and Truth,
the fire grows brighter.

As it consumes all that does not belong in the Kingdom
it's flames burn brighter
and the light within grows more brilliant.

Cast into the fire any thought or possession
which does not serve a Kingdom purpose
and allow your life to shine brightly with the Light of God.

The following poem has many thoughts to inspire each of us
to experience Kingdom Living.

You are invited to read the poem in its
entirety as often as you wish,
and then take one stanza a day upon which to meditate.

You may repeat the stanza several times and
carry it in your heart throughout the day.
Use the *Notes* page to record any thoughts that come to you
in response to each stanza.

It is my hope that you will be encouraged
to ponder, meditate and pray.
May you find the Kingdom of Heaven
within your heart in every moment.

Love, Marcia

Today I will choose peace above all else.
I will live in harmony with others.

Today I will remain calm and
Will hold silence at my center.

Today I will not worry.
I will trust the universal wisdom.

Today I will not judge anyone or anything.
I will accept all as it is.

Today I will not hurry.
I will allow my life to unfold gracefully.

Today I will not dwell on self.
I will reach out with vision towards others.

Today I will not withhold love.
I will choose compassion as my only response.

Today I will not dwell in fear.
I will remember that pure love is all there is.

Today I will not question my potential.
I will remember that I am a powerful, spiritual being.

Today I will live fully in each moment.
I will not be bound by the illusion of past and future.

Today I will call out to God.
I will find the eternal kingdom of heaven within my being.

Today I will remember I am not separate from others.
I will rejoice in my oneness with God and all of creation.

Today I will be myself,
The pure, loving divine spirit,
created and sustained by the love of God.

NOTES

One Way a Day
Deepening My Commitment
to Kingdom Living

NOTES

**1. Today I will choose peace above all else.
I will live in harmony with others.**

What are some of the things in my life that I allow
to take away my peace?

Being caught in traffic
Losing something
Running late
A comment someone makes

Today I recognize that I can choose my response
to every circumstance in my life
and today I will choose peace above all else.
I will take time to observe my emotions
and I will choose to respond in peace
instead of reacting quickly in frustration or anger.
I will live in harmony with others.
I will not be the source of discord
in any of my relationships.
I recognize that peace begins with me
and I take full responsibility
for creating peace in my own life

**Today I will choose peace above all else.
I will live in harmony with others.**

NOTES

**2. Today I will remain calm.
I will hold silence at my center.**

Today I will take time to quiet myself –
to quiet my busy thoughts
and allow myself to experience silence.
I will observe and acknowledge
all the thoughts and emotions
that arise during the day
and breathing deeply
I will slowly let them go-
allowing them to slip away
- one by one -
until I feel the calm at the center of my being.
Continuing to breathe slowly and deeply,
I will choose to hold this silence
at my center throughout the day.
Anytime I find myself moving away from this calm
I will once again breathe deeply
and allow unwanted energy to dissolve
and I will enter into my desired silence.

**Today I will remain calm.
I will hold silence at my center.**

NOTES

3. Today I will not worry.
I will trust the Universal wisdom.

Worry cannot change the outcome
so what does it benefit my mind, heart and soul to worry?
Worry offers no protection or solution to apparent problems.
Worry does not enhance vision rather it blocks our sight.
So today I will choose to trust the wisdom that sustains my life.
I will trust the Universal Wisdom
that guides the stars and planets;
that changes the seasons;
that tells a flower how to grow;
that teaches the birds to fly in synchronized flight;
that causes my body to rebuild itself
day by day and year after year.
I do not doubt that this Universal Wisdom
can keep the Earth spinning and I will not fall off.
So why would I worry about any circumstance
that arises in my life?

Today I will not worry.
I will trust the Universal wisdom.

NOTES

**4. Today I will not judge anyone or anything.
I will accept all as it is.**

I will suspend judgment in each moment
and will choose instead to observe.
I will release, from my narrow mind,
thoughts of criticism
and allow my awareness
to expand and open to loving thoughts of acceptance.
I will not form unnecessary opinions
about people and things around me today.
I will stay aware
that what may at first appear as a difference or dislike
may represent a part of myself
I prefer not to allow into my consciousness
and I will invite inner vision
to be present in each moment.
I will accept all as it appears,
knowing that as I gently allow everything
to be part of the natural flow of life
(bring it to the level of awareness)
I then make change a possibility.
In accepting what is, I allow things to shift
and recognize that the Universe
continues to unfold gracefully around me.
My struggle to change things that I do not wish to accept
results in rigidity, which ultimately blocks the flow of life
and makes even more difficult that which I desire to change.
I choose to release those judgments
and step into the peaceful flow of acceptance.

**Today I will not judge anyone or anything.
I will accept all as it is.**

NOTES

5. Today I will not hurry.
I will allow my life to unfold gracefully.

I will take time to quiet myself and to focus on a point
of inner stillness and silence.
I will allow timelessness to flow through me
and will reconnect with the wheel of eternity
where there is no beginning and no end
and all that is, is Now.
I will step into the River of Life
trusting that I will be carried
by the ever-present current of Love.
I will allow each moment of my life
to unfold gracefully
as a beautiful Lily upon the water.
I will cease to rush through each moment
and will allow each moment its place within me.
I will not hurry -
I will stay aware that within each moment
is the Life that I am choosing
and I will pause to reflect upon the river
as it flows all around me.

**Today I will not hurry.
I will allow my life to unfold gracefully.**

NOTES

**6. Today I will not dwell on self.
I will reach out with vision towards others.**

I will open my eyes
to see the hearts around me
and reach out a helping hand.
I will speak a kind word of encouragement.
moving quickly to offer help.
I will not strive to keep myself the center of attention
but rather open my center
and allow my attention to flow lovingly
into the lives of those around me.
I will decide now to see others through eyes of love
and will recognize the blessing
both in giving and receiving.
I will hold the vision of the divine perfection of each soul
and offer this vision to all I meet.
I will reach out and extend the vision of love to all.

**Today I will not dwell on self.
I will reach out with vision towards others.**

NOTES

**7. Today I will not withhold love.
I will choose compassion as my only response.**

I will see everything in my life
either as an expression of love or as a call for love
and I will respond with love.
I will love those who do not appear to love me
as well as those who do.
I will love those who appear to be against me
as well as those who support me.
I will not base my decision for love
upon the words and actions of others.
Rather I will open my heart
to the unconditional love of the Spirit of God
and allow pure love to flow through me
penetrating into the circle of family and friends
and flowing out into the community and the world.
I will love without expectation,
knowing that the Spirit is the only Source of love
and as I give love I am blessed by love.
As I become love
I find myself in the heavenly Kingdom of love.

**Today I will not withhold love.
I will choose compassion as my only response**

NOTES

**8. Today I will not dwell in fear.
I will remember that pure Love is all there is.**

I will face the shadow and call it by name,
thus bringing it into the light.
I will recognize that fear is an illusion and has no substance.
Perfect Love illuminates and casts out fear
and I will choose to receive Love,
give Love and be Love
in every moment.
Fear can only exist if Love is not present
and since Love is eternal it is everywhere.
So fear(darkness)
comes from my decision
to block love (light) from my reality
which in itself is an illusion
since nothing can separate us from the Love of God.
Behind every cloak and curtain of darkness and fear
lies a longing for love.
If I can, in each moment, bring love to the forefront
it will shine its light into the darkness
and reveal that both darkness and fear were not real.
For in the light of Love there can be no darkness
and fear loses all its appearance of power.
I will hold pure love in my heart
and send out nothing but love from me.

**Today I will not dwell in fear.
I will remember that pure Love is all there is.**

NOTES

**9. Today I will not question my potential.
I will remember that I am a powerful spiritual being.**

I will hold no limiting thoughts of myself.
I will believe that all things are possible.
I will remember that I am a powerful spiritual being,
connected to the eternal creative energy of God
and I will release any blocks in my life
that would restrict the flow of God-energy.
I will not doubt my potential,
knowing that it is a reflection of God's power
and that with God nothing is impossible.
I recognize that God's loving, creating, powerful energy
is the source of all abundance.
And because we are created and sustained by God,
we are all connected to this abundance.
We do not have to ask for it.
We need only remember that it is also present within us.
As we open our minds and hearts to the Spirit of God,
we free our spirit to be one with God again.
And all things are possible in our life
when our connection to God is clear.

**Today I will not question my potential.
I will remember that I am a powerful spiritual being.**

NOTES

**10. Today I will live fully in each moment.
I will not be bound by the illusion of past and future.**

I will choose to experience Now.
I will bring to this moment
no thoughts and images from the past
that do not serve me in the present.
Nor will I fill this moment
with thoughts of what is yet to come.
I will direct my focus to the task at hand:
I will listen to my heart now.
I will stay alert and available
to what others are expressing now,
and in each moment
I will create an experience of love and beauty.
I will not put off until tomorrow what I can do today
and I will not bring forward into today
thoughts of what I did not accomplish yesterday.
In each moment I will see what truly is,
and I will release the illusions of past and future.

**Today I will live fully in each moment.
I will not be bound by the illusion of past and future.**

NOTES

11. Today I will call out to God.
I will find the eternal kingdom of heaven within my being.

Today I will honour my desire to stay connected to my Source.
I will call out to God and will remain open
to receive God in every moment.
I will unlock the doors and windows of my inner chamber
and will sit quietly, ready to receive God.
I will release anything I have been holding on to
and prepare my heart
for the loving embrace of my Creator.
I will find the kingdom of Heaven within my very being.
As I allow Love to flow in,
it brings with it the fullness of the Kingdom.
I am filled by the presence of my Creator;
this Love flows out through every window and door
of my inner chamber into my body,
into my life, into my world…
and I find myself carried effortlessly
upon the River of Life.
The Kingdom of Heaven
has entered my Heart
and expands around me.

Today I will call out to God.
I will find the eternal kingdom of heaven within my being.

NOTES

**12. Today I will remember I am not separate from others.
I will rejoice in my oneness with God and all of creation.**

Today I will recognize
that we are all pearls on the same infinite necklace,
held together by a long cord of Love.
The cord is God's Spirit,
which flows through each of us,
connecting us with the eternal strand of Life.
I will rejoice in my connection with others
and in my connection with God.
I will rejoice in the oneness of creation with the Creator.
I will recognize that if we choose
to fill the spaces between each pearl with fear and illusion
then we lose our vision of the necklace as a whole
and can be deceived into thinking each pearl is separate
and not connected to the others.
But no matter how far we may try to separate ourselves
we cannot sever the chord which runs through us.
It is the cord of Spirit, which sustains us and indeed IS us.

**Today I will remember I am not separate from others.
I will rejoice in my oneness with God and all of creation.**

NOTES

**13. Today I will be myself, a pure, loving, divine spirit,
created and sustained by the love of God.**

Today I will not work at "being",
rather I will allow my being to activate my life.
I will allow the divine, Spirit energy
to flow freely through me
and allow myself
to be sustained by the love of God.
I will let go of all effort
to be something apart from God
and will reconnect with the essence
of who I really am.
I will know that God dwells in me
and gives me His Spirit in every moment
and I will be myself, a pure, loving, divine spirit,
created and sustained by the Love of God.
The sustaining power of God
is available to us at all times.
God does not change
so when we experience change
it is within our own perception.

**Today I will be myself, a pure, loving, divine spirit,
created and sustained by the love of God.**

NOTES

The Kingdom of Heaven requires neither
a building nor infrastructure.
It exhibits no superficial, outward characteristics.
Neither are the requirements for entry difficult or complicated
The Kingdom of Heaven is in the heart that humbly seeks it.
The heart of the Kingdom is in you.

BIBLIOGRAPHY

All These Things Added James Allen
The Bible NIV (New International Version)
The Kingdom Within John A. Sanford
Living A Course in Miracles: An Essential Guide
to the Classic Text Jon Mundy PhD
Writing In The Sand. Thomas Moore

Printed in the United States
By Bookmasters